ALL ABOUT THE OZONE LAYER

EFFECTS ON HUMAN, ANIMAL AND PLANT HEALTH

Environment Books | Children's Environment Books

Speedy Publishing LLC
40 E. Main St. #1156
Newark, DE 19711
www.speedypublishing.com

Copyright © 2017

n this book, we're going to talk about the ozone layer and its effects on people, animals, and plants. So, let's get right to it!

The decrease of ozone, called ozone depletion, is a huge environmental problem, one that affects everyone on Earth. Our Sun is about 93 million miles away from us and yet its heat and warmth come to Earth. Without the Sun, we couldn't live on Earth.

Rays from the Sun also contain ultraviolet rays, called UV rays for short. We need some UV rays because they help our bodies create Vitamin D. However, too much UV is very dangerous.

Outer space view of clouds over planet earth.

WHAT IS OZONE?

Regular oxygen, the type we breathe, is made up of two oxygen atoms and is written as O_2. Regular oxygen has no color. It also has no odor. Ozone, also called trioxygen, is an unstable gas. It's toxic and it has a pale blue color. It also has a very strong smell. It's made of three oxygen molecules and is written as O_3. Ozone is formed when ultraviolet light hits oxygen. The UV light splits the oxygen atoms and once separated from the O_2, the individual oxygen atoms latch on to other O_2 molecules to create O_3.

GOOD OZONE VERSUS BAD OZONE

Ozone occurs naturally, but it occurs very rarely as a result of natural processes. For every 10 million molecules of air, there are only 3 molecules of natural ozone. Even though it's rare, ozone plays an important role in the safety of our atmosphere. Depending on where the ozone is located in our atmosphere, it can have helpful or harmful effects.

Ozone Molecule.

Sun

UV protection by the ozone layer.

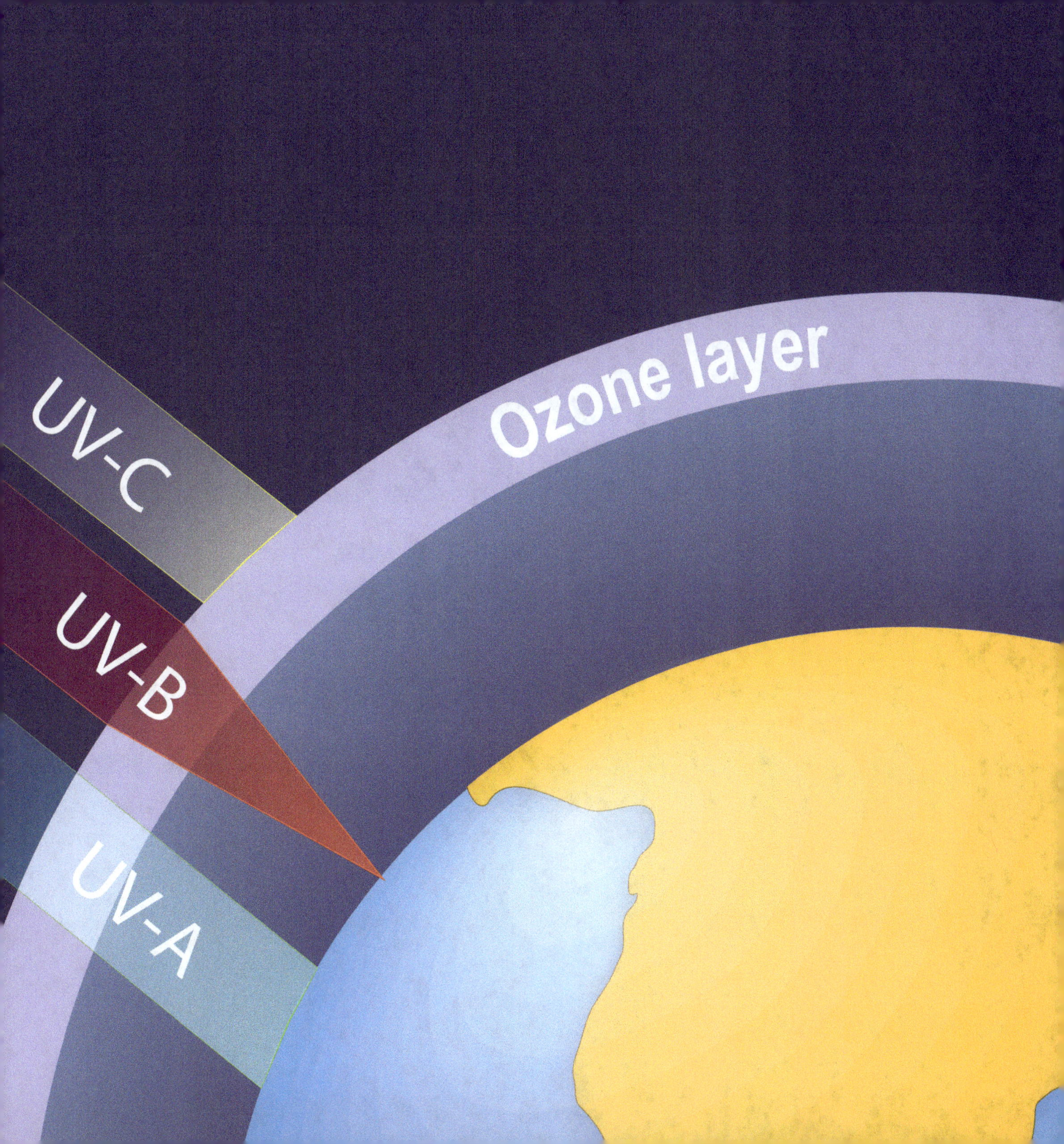

Ozone layer
UV-C
UV-B
UV-A

GOOD OZONE
IN THE
STRATOSPHERE

magine that you are traveling through the layers of the atmosphere on Earth. From Earth's surface to about 6 to 10 miles (10 to 17 kilometers) up, you encounter the first part of the atmosphere, which is called the troposphere.

This is the part of the atmosphere where we breathe. Walking on the street, going mountain climbing, riding in a gas balloon, or operating a small aircraft would take place in the troposphere.

ATMOSPHERE

EXOSPHERE
>700 TO 190,000 KM

EXOBASE
>700 TO 1,000 KM

THERMOSPHERE
80 TO 700 KM

KARMAN LINE
100 KM

MESOSPHERE
50 TO 80 KM

STRATOSPHER
12 TO 50 KM

OZONE LAYER
20 TO 30 KM

TROPOSHERE
0 TO 12 KM

The next layer of Earth's atmosphere after the troposphere is the stratosphere. It stretches up above the troposphere for approximately 30 miles or 50 kilometers.

It's here in the lower portion of the stratosphere where 90% of the ozone in our atmosphere resides. It forms a very thin layer usually about 12 to 19 miles (20 to 30 kilometers) above the Earth. The thickness of this ozone layer varies from season to season and also varies based on its location on our planet.

The natural ozone in this layer is vitally important. It shields the Earth from the effects of too much ultraviolet light. Ozone molecules absorb this potentially harmful UV light, which can cause damaging sunburn and ultimately skin cancer in humans. It can also cause damage to the eyes in the form of cataracts. Damaging UV light is called UV-B.

Without the help of the ozone layer, UV-B radiation would come through the atmosphere and cause harm not just to humans, but to other animals and plants as well. Many experimental studies have been done that demonstrate the damage done by too much UV-B.

Too much exposure to UV-B reduces the size and quality of crops, which animals and humans depend on for food. It also hurts phytoplankton, which is vital to the food chain in our oceans. If the ozone continues to get thinner, the consequences could be disastrous to life on Earth.

As the ozone absorbs the UV-B it also generates heat, which actually helps to create the stratosphere. The ozone layer plays a dual role. It protects the troposphere from too much harmful UV-B and it generates heat as it absorbs the UV-B, helping to form the stratosphere's structure. As you go up to higher altitudes in the stratosphere, the temperature increases.

Blue mountains.

BAD OZONE IN THE TROPOSPHERE

About 10% of the ozone of our atmosphere exists in the troposphere. Ozone is very beneficial in the stratosphere, but in the troposphere it's toxic to living things. In summary, the ozone in the stratosphere keeps us safe from harmful UV-B, but in the troposphere the effects of ozone are toxic.

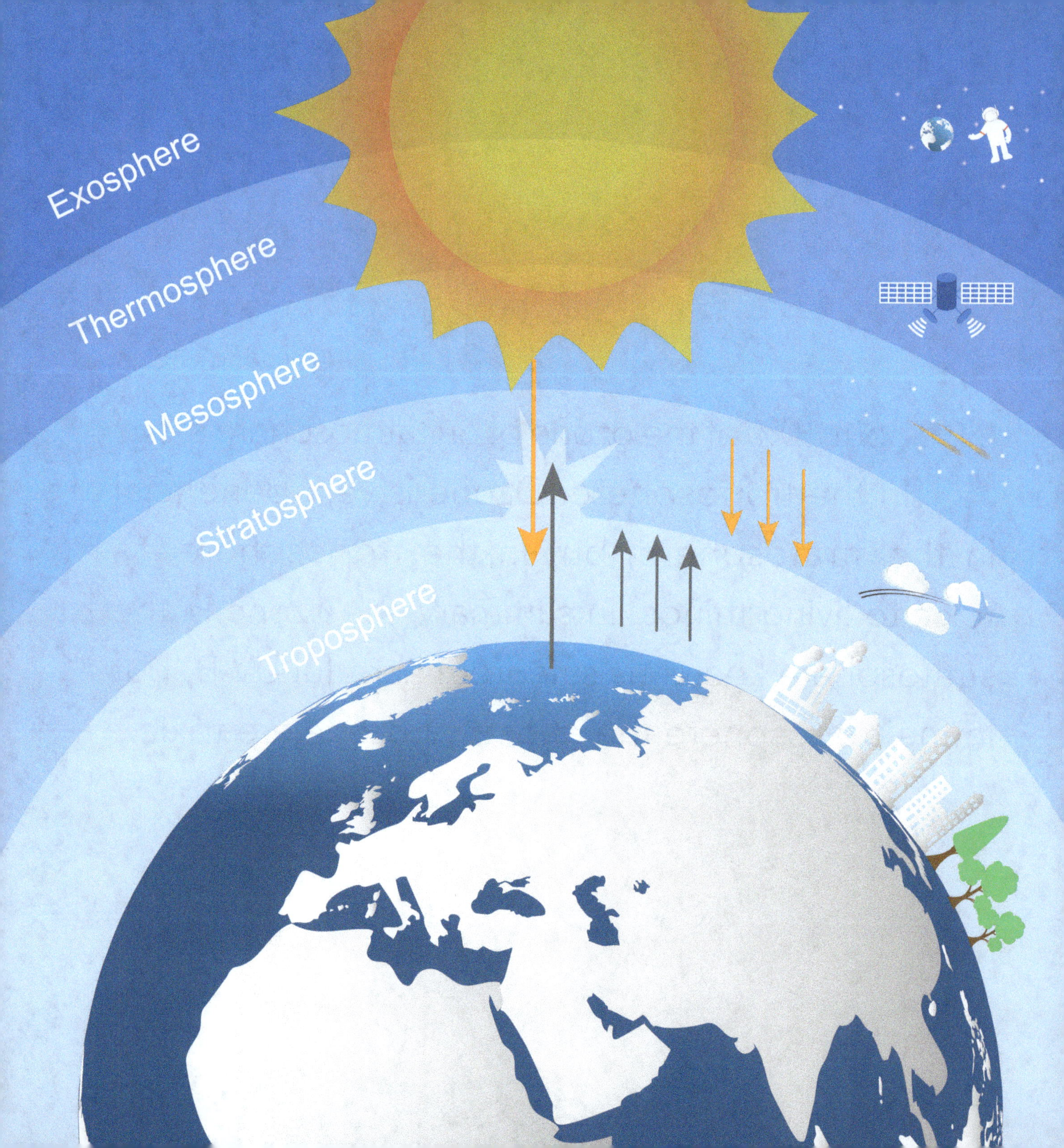

Exosphere
Thermosphere
Mesosphere
Stratosphere
Troposphere

WHY IS THE AMOUNT OF OZONE IN THE GOOD OZONE LAYER DECREASING?

The ozone layer provides a natural "sunscreen" for our troposphere. However, the ozone is getting much thinner in spots than it used to be. Pollution of the atmosphere is caused by many different factors. However, in the case of the ozone layer, environmentalists have found that there is a specific reason this is happening. The depletion of the ozone layer is being caused specifically by types of chemicals called chlorofluorocarbons, abbreviated as CFCs.

The main layers atmosphere of earth.

WHERE DO CFCs COME FROM?

CFCs come from human manufacturing. For example, the refrigerants used in air conditioning and refrigerators that keep things cool are CFCs. Fire extinguishers and spray cans contain CFCs as well. So do many types of foams as well as solvents and soaps used in manufacturing.

Hand with aerosol can.

After two to five years of being in the atmosphere, CFCs are carried up into the stratosphere by wind. Once sunlight reacts with the CFCs it breaks them up and the molecules of chlorine are released. Then the chlorine reacts with the ozone and begins to destroy it. The continued chemical reactions deplete even more ozone. Just one atom of chlorine can cause the ultimate destruction of over 100,000 molecules of ozone.

THE BUCKET ANALOGY

You can think about how ozone depletion works, if you imagine a leaky bucket. The rays of the Sun produce ozone by reacting with oxygen. Natural chemicals such as nitrogen, chlorine, and hydrogen destroy some of the ozone molecules, but this natural process of creation and destruction stays in balance.

This is where CFCs come in. They cause destruction of the ozone and have now thrown the natural balance of creation and destruction, causing more ozone to be destroyed than created.

Ozone logo on the sky with reflection.

WHAT IS THE OZONE HOLE?

The ozone layer varies during the seasons and it also varies by latitude. In the 70s it was discovered that the ozone was thinner in the latitudes of the Arctic and Antarctic. This huge area of thinner ozone layer was estimated to be the size of the continental US. It was mostly observed during the spring months. During the winter months, temperatures at the poles can drop below -100 degrees Fahrenheit.

There are thin clouds that have concentrated mixtures of ice as well as nitric and sulphuric acids. These begin a series of chemical reactions that release CFCs and by spring a lot of the ozone has been thinned. As the spring goes on, temperatures get warmer, and as the ice melts the ozone layer begins to return to a better level.

Hazardous waste - broken fridges containing cfc, danger to the ozone.

High concrete chimney emits CO₂ into the atmosphere.
CO₂

BANNING OF CFCs

In the 70s, two scientists, named Mario Molina and Sherry Rowland, discovered the connection between CFCs and the reduction and thinning of the ozone layer.

Regulation of products using CFCs was started, but it took until 1987 before a treaty was signed to stop CFC creation and use worldwide. The goal of this treaty was to completely get rid of CFCs by 2000.

Sunglasses against the sun.

LONG-TERM HEALTH EFFECTS

CFCs are measured in the atmosphere by balloons as well as satellites and aircraft. Unfortunately, CFCs last a long time, for up to a century. So, even if 100% of CFC use stopped tomorrow, the ozone layer will more than likely continue to be affected for some time, causing risk of skin cancer. Always use sunscreen when you go outside and are in the sun for any length of time. A good quality pair of sunglasses that reduces UV exposure will help your eyes be protected as well.

Always use sunscreen when you go outside and are in the sun for any length of time. A good quality pair of sunglasses that reduces UV exposure will help your eyes be protected as well.

WHAT CAN WE DO ABOUT THE DEPLETION OF GOOD OZONE?

We can't do much about CFCs that are already in the atmosphere, but there are a few things that we can pay attention to.

Refrigerators that were manufactured before 1995 sometimes contain refrigerants that were made with CFCs. Buy a refrigerator that doesn't use CFC refrigerant and make sure to follow environmental guidelines on how to get rid of the old refrigerator.

POWER SLEEP
TIMER RUN

Air conditioners that were manufactured prior to 1994, use Freon, which is made from CFCs. If you have one of these, you should buy a new environmentally safer air conditioner. The new chemicals in air conditioners are called HCFCs and even though they are better than CFCs, they still cause some ozone depletion, so the best thing to do is use your air conditioning as little as possible.

Foam products frequently contain CFCs. Instead of using foam to package materials crumple up old newspapers or use other types of environmentally friendly packing materials.

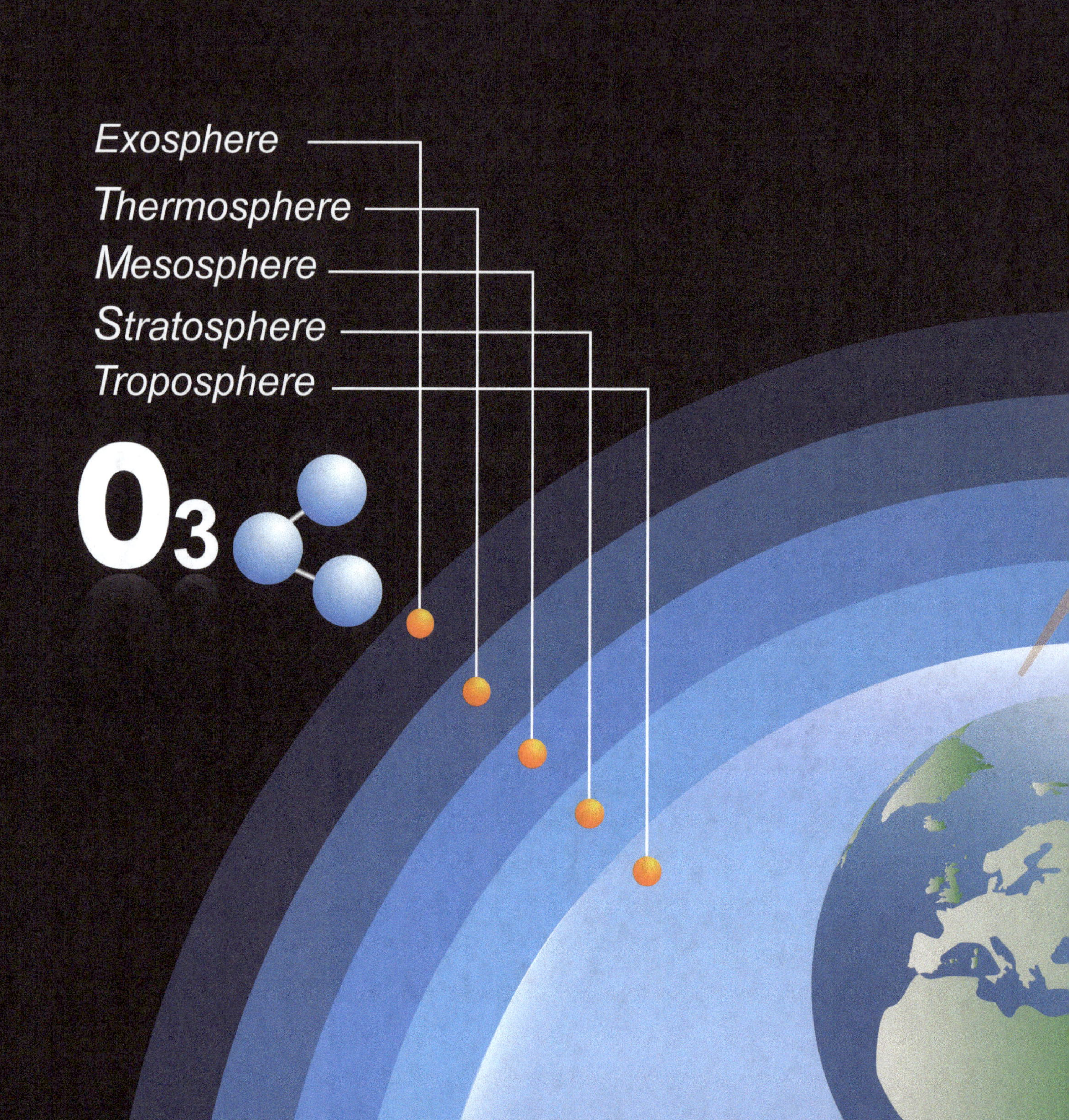

Exosphere
Thermosphere
Mesosphere
Stratosphere
Troposphere
O₃

Some people have wondered why we can't find a way to produce our own ozone gas to replace what's been lost. The Sun is very powerful and it creates ozone over a very long period of time and using a huge amount of energy. It's just not possible for us to do that with current technologies.

Awesome! Now you know more about the ozone layer and what you can do to help. You can find more Environment books from Baby Professor by searching the website of your favorite book retailer.

Visit
BABY PROFESSOR
EDUCATION KIDS
www.BabyProfessorBooks.com
to download Free Baby Professor eBooks
and view our catalog of new and exciting
Children's Books